What Is
Beyond Us

ALSO BY KAREN FISH

The Cedar Canoe

What Is Beyond Us

POEMS BY

KAREN FISH

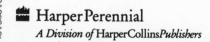

HarperPerennial
A Division of HarperCollinsPublishers

The quotes at the end of the poem "Paradise" are from an article by Guy Davenport, "Henri Rousseau," first published in *Antaeus,* Number 54 (New York: Ecco Press, 1985).

The poem *"Egypt in Flaubert's Time"* was inspired by an article entitled "Egypt in Flaubert's Time: An Exhibition of the First Photographers, 1839–1860" by André and Marie-Thérèse Jammes, published in *Aperture,* Number 78 (Millerton, New York: 1977).

The quotes at the end of *"Egypt in Flaubert's Time"* are from *The Voices of Silence* by André Malraux, translated by Stuart Gilbert (Princeton: Princeton University Press, 1978).

The poem *"The Fire's Hypnotic Flickering"* was inspired by *Camille: The Life of Camille Claudel, Rodin's Muse and Mistress* by Reine-Marie Paris (New York: Seaver Books, Henry Holt, 1984).

The quotation from David St. John is from the book *No Heaven* (Boston: Houghton Mifflin, 1985) and is reprinted by permission of the author.

HarperCollins Books may be purchased for educational, business, or sales promotional use. For information, please write: Special Markets Department, HarperCollins Publishers, Inc., 10 East 53rd Street, New York, NY 10022.

FIRST EDITION

Designed by Alma Hochhauser Orenstein

Library of Congress Cataloging-in-Publication Data
Fish, Karen, 1959–
    What is beyond us : poems / by Karen Fish.—1st ed.
      p. cm.
    ISBN 0-06-055336-7 / ISBN 0-06-096953-9 (pbk.)
    I. Title.
    PS3556.I77W48   1992   92-52630
    811'.54—dc20

---

92 93 94 95 96 CC/HC 10 9 8 7 6 5 4 3 2 1
92 93 94 95 96 CC/HC 10 9 8 7 6 5 4 3 2 1 (pbk.)

ACKNOWLEDGMENTS

Some of the poems have been published in the following magazines, to whose editors grateful acknowledgment is made:

The American Poetry Review: "Swans," "What Is Beyond Us,"
      "Woods Hole: Cape Cod," "The Back Room,"
      "Paradise," "Letter from the Modern World."

The Denver Quarterly: "The Beginning."

The Florida Review: "When the Soul Leaves the Body."

Hayden's Ferry Review: "Egypt in Flaubert's Time," "The Fire's
      Hypnotic Flickering."

Indiana Review: "December," "The Annunciation."

North American Review: "The Middle Ages."

The Partisan Review: "The Tub."

The Paris Review: "The Dreams."

Pushcart Prize XV: The Best of the Small Presses: "What Is
      Beyond Us" was reprinted.

Completion of this manuscript was aided by grants from the Maryland State Arts Council and Loyola College faculty development grants. I am especially grateful to Stephen Berg and David St. John for their constant encouragement.

And for criticism that helped to shape these poems, my special thanks to Dan McGuiness, JoEllen Kwiatek, and Sheila Gillooly.

—for Tim Stapleton

Rarely, Rarely
Comest Thou, Spirit
of Delight!

—Percy Bysshe Shelley

CONTENTS

| ONE |

| TWO |

| *THREE* |

One

Paradise

Our souls therefore, which are one,
    Though I must go, endure not yet
A breach, but an expansion,
    Like gold to airy thinness beat.

—JOHN DONNE

FOR MY UNCLE, PETER, 1936–1978

Being modern, we described that feeling,
the day, the hour being too good—
the sun unleashed & slack
above us as cinematic. We said, we felt like we were
    created,
viewed—it was one of those rare moments for us as
    modern characters—
we actually stood outside ourselves
and imagined how we'd look.
We felt like main characters but it was probably just
God's green eye focused to a patience on us.

There were trees stroked into polished, twisted
forms on the side of the hill, burnished like stones by the
    wind
or glass by water. The grass was scorched gold
and the hillside such a luxury on the eye—easy—
a few trees, a hawk doing a figure-eight, deer invisible
but present in the thick bramble of the lower valley.

Starlings passed by like fish in formation.
Look, I said and pointed, *a flock of birds flying in the shape*
of a garden spade, as we spoke
starting and stopping. When we fell

to rest, we had the posture of those thrown,
posture of those painted into allegory,
with the sky just good government behind us.
When we did rest it was the incline we used
as a bench. We didn't know we were tormented.
We were instead lovely, related by blood.
This was before we made our mistakes. This was before
I was an adult, still pretty as a cat, lazy & unself-
            conscious . . .
this was before you died early.
Is this the awful truth: are all betrayals as important
as the famous ones?

And I was there with you & surely it had so much to do
with dilution, this falling into each other.
It is always like this: *love*.
It is like waking in an unfamiliar room, waking fast
and for seconds you don't know yourself
& it is a relief. You have dissolved—forgotten your own
            particulars
and you love deeply that amnesia like just broken sleep,
you wonder where you are as you survey the hillside,
the strange trees moving in the breeze, the birds that fly
in the shape of a shovel, the light's position, the grillwork
of shadow across the path.
And like the Impressionists *who kept their purpose secret:*
being unaware of it: the idea of transition—
we move up the hill, the light heavy,
making us sleepy, exhausted,
the light heavy as crowns upon our heads.

Irony

for Greg

I always think of something like metal first, a hand gripping
a cold pipe, or railing which is so cold the bare skin
of the hand sticks, adheres for a second.
There is always a story, just as there is always someone
who drinks too much and tells tales.
It was my fourteenth birthday and I remember it all
like a lover with a photographic memory recalls a physical
        body.
I could say—*the net-work of foam in a wave*
looks the same as the veins of a leaf
held up in sunlight.
And maybe that is what I was thinking
standing there at that window in the wood clapboard house
on the high dune at the ocean's beginning, twilight
flooding the house—night seeming to assemble particle
by particle. Somewhere in the back of the house
was my brother singing to ward off a fear of darkness.
My father fell asleep full of scotch, standing
at the ocean's edge. My father collapsed there like a shadow
of a cloud falling over a hillside in summer.
The surrounding dunes were empty, the long beach grass
bowed to a wind and I was paused at the window watching
        my mother,
a woman who didn't know she was being watched—
walk deafly toward the sea, her scarf pulsing in the breeze.

Why is the witness always so embarrassed?
Is there really guilt in seeing?
This seeing is captivity. My mother walking

toward an ocean and its loud chant. And this is what
I remember, over and over:
my mother bent down, buckled her hands
around my father's wrists like handcuffs and pulled him
       back
from the tide and then sat down beside his body . . .
black smoke rose like streamers off the beach from
       clambakes
down shore. The house whistled in the weather,
and I watched them till their features darkened and
my parents became anonymous, till the credible moon
rose obedient as if called
from that far horizon
and the millions of what seemed to be decorative,
domestic stars showed design.

When the Soul Leaves the Body

FOR DREW LEDER

When the soul leaves the body does it surface like a
    swimmer
who needs a breath badly, coming to the lid of sky
    exhausted,
eye-level with the wavering net of pattern, light and
    shadow . . .
When the soul leaves the body does it jump like a person
    from
a spun car through black smoke before the vehicle explodes
and stops . . .
Is it just another place, another white room flooded with
the clarity of light, the edge of vision . . .
Must we give up our tricks then—
the slick man his rhythmic voice,
the woman who can only use her eyes, their maneuvers—
do we drop them like a grocery bag that gives out at the
    bottom
and walk on?
Do we go ahead, to where we were before,
where contradictions become complete
like the tree merging with its reflection
to the dark intoxication which is not the self.
Will I hear my own voice—softly through the dark say,
just tell me what you want me to do.

Pastoral

The sequence of leaves across the river fills,
leaves catching the wind like spinnakers.
The auctioneer's voice comes like a yodel
from the opposite shore. There is a public sale,
but the actual bidding, his words, are lost
because of distance—instead it is a song.
That shore is gold and flames
in this late afternoon chance, slant of light.

I forget momentarily, then remember—
much like a person learning, accepting an illness;
guarding myself from your absence.
There is nothing abstract about loss;
it is a real door that opens.
I pace the hours which are rooms and stand
at the window. A heron makes a sick wounding cry
from the salt marsh, the reeds tremble, swallows
wind out from nests under the dock in a folly.
As a child near night, my companions and I, would play
outside, taking turns swinging each other.
We would try to stay, struck in the pose we were thrown
into—*statues*.

Woods Hole: Cape Cod

FOR ILONA McGUINESS

This landscape is not metaphor.
I want the actual thing, a particular sky.
Sky as door and then the sun—
usually a sloppy, bright garland wreath stuck
to that particular black nail.
The nail's the only solid thing from heaven that I've seen.
See, the rash of rain peppering the surface of the bay.
Maude Gifford's husband in a shallow oyster boat
scissoring his way between grass islands on stilts.

This is the view taken away.
Let's say the land is sold. Let's say
the elderly are moved to town,
placed somewhere to be cared for—away
from the stoves, the burners they forget to extinguish,
from the stairs—the hours, the days holding
their frail bones in place.
The land as inheritance, stolen and badly managed.
It was my dead father's sonnet—
This is what you will receive
This is what you will receive
receive

The moonlight searches out the bedroom
where my grandfather's father was born, first cried.
The stars just heads of light
between the splayed limbs of old trees.

The ground I speak of—my afterlife, the daydream
my father wanted to pass to me
like a white envelope, better than cash.
The trees are struck to a rumor of hills,
clouds tethered to the distant shadow of ocean.
The fishing boats arrive strung with lights,
and Portuguese families crowd the breakfast bar before
        dawn.
The sun is always the soothsayer, the rocks circling
the lighthouse, suspect as ever. Nothing changes
good and evil, certainly not time.

The moan of the engines, heavy barges
dredging our notion of the bay—making it deeper.
Geese fly over the house, a hook
again and again, catching only the season.

And it is twilight when I am most sympathetic
thinking of the farmers without their farms, without
the long walk to the mailbox,
their sun plunging into the barn roof, night
after night. It is always twilight
when I imagine the demolition of the present tense,
the blue shadow of the homestead coupled to
the lawn no longer mine.
The water view, the moon a twirling
bright weather vane on the roof of the house.
Twilight, when I miss the black hollyhock,
blue larkspur.

The Beginning

Much in the same manner as the eye being led
skillfully into a painting   starting at the thin
beige   nicely   modeled wrist   then following an arm
in toward the center to a face hanging in front of
an apricot sky
getting out again is no matter
futile as bailing a boat
that allows more salt water in
through a gash in the hull than two arms
could possibly bail out
in a given afternoon

It is not to be measured   like a creek bed, speculated
even accurately as the dark line left along the side of the
        bank's wall
where the stream might have coursed last week after rain
muddy and far from transparent
Much in the same manner as the eye moving
into a painting   love starts
and following the wrist is an act of faith
a commitment   to have gotten the viewer   even that far
toward a dear face

Klara

To be lost is only a failure of memory.
　　　　　　—Margaret Atwood

1. Norway

The late afternoon sky burns like a ship fire far off.
My great-grandmother is walking past the fishing boats,
a considerable distance from the commotion, from the
　　　　　whales
that are dead and hanging heavily off the end of the runway
　　　　to shore.
She is recently engaged, and her fiancé
stands on a steamship looking the opposite direction,
watching the baggage nets dangle over the deck,
the space between the dock and red hull
where the dark water splashes, and bits of paper and wood
　　　　float.

Snow is piled everywhere, the horses are muttering
and wagging their heads. The moon is high in the
　　　　afternoon sky,
white and sturdy behind the government office buildings.
Klara is walking home, red-faced, away from the ships,
through the city's pink air.

This day will end just like a flame pinched out—
her mother's thin fingers extinguishing the dinner candles
in a tail of smoke, after everything has been cleared away.
And it seems as if he has already been gone so long, her
      lover,
not just a few hours out into the dark water
under thousands of stars.

Just beyond the horizon, the lights of Norway—*music
he can almost hear*. The months ahead just pages, pages
in a book not yet read . . . those terrible white pages
to be turned slowly, slowly the way Klara's mother
lowers the dinner plate each evening in front
of her father's face.

2. Missouri

From the steamed windows you can see the yellow fields,
the pigeon-gray sky, the black smoke that rides over the
        train
in lashed bundles.
Klara is dressed in black, her eyes are closed
and she is sitting on blue mohair.
I could tell you that she has no money,
is thinking of a huge pond in Norway where she used to
        ice-skate.
She can smell a mixture of pine & verbena.
She is watching herself skate, once, twice
around the perimeter—it seems colder moving her stiff legs
over the far side of the white pond.
People in dark clothes skate in pairs and the children lace
awkward chains and fly off the ice into snowbanks.
A small girl slides up behind, knocking Klara behind the
        knees,
kicking them both to the ice. The fire drum and its flames
hang sideways as does the shore.

3. Woods Hole: Cape Cod

The Klara you see now, standing in front of the small
      harbor,
still has no money. The small blonde girl, who is squinting,
standing next to a pile of baggage and watching a tiny
      sailboat
weave in and out toward the mouth of the bay, is her
      daughter.
I have no memory of this but—
Klara did not marry the man looking the opposite direction
five years before. He wrote and called it off.
She met and married someone else from America
and had his daughter and then sat vigil at his bedside.

It was a kind of astonishment, her hands wringing
the cold towels while he turned pale, cold as the
      ice-infested
water beyond some distant window.

I could say then, that her mother-in-law cheated her
of the inheritance in Missouri.
The green clapboard house behind her now
with the two women's faces hanging like inward reflections,
like moons watching from the second-story windows,
is the house of the only other person she knows in
      America.
She got here kneading men's backs like hundreds of loaves
      of bread
and the man that stood on the steamship years ago
is down at the club. His sisters will take her in,
they have already realized who she is,

this woman standing between the house and harbor
in a glare that pushes the few boats to invisibility.
She waits to face their brother again.
And my great-grandfather who is now drinking scotch
will love her again.

This is an exhaustion like the eye constantly miscalculating
the horizon . . .
as the ferry churns the water and disappears
toward the islands. I am no different,
the great-granddaughter taught to seek
the heart's flaw & love the flaw. Slowly, the past returns—
I watch the water, the tiny waves,
till a whirlpool begins, the color of the water changes,
and a sandbar emerges, slow rising
from the tide which recedes.

Two

The Annunciation

As if what most women manage weren't miracle enough.
Cutting loose the thing made. The bridge from heaven
is, of course, the woman's body.
If men are jealous of anything
it is the everyday miracle of ordinary birth.
Something springing from nothing,
the reminder of the animal; the thing so surely
of this world made, one's place in it.

How shocking to see the real thing.
How bright and flashy the actual colors . . .
not those muted, gray reproductions in *The History of Art*.
In any depiction the architecture is all wrong,
too updated, recognizable.

The road outside dries to chalk,
and the mule, the man of wood are to come later; also,
the bridge of palms. For now, it is just the daylight sky,
the moon frozen in the center, bright, reflective.
Sunlight so heavy she has to sleep.
She knows what she knows is not a dream.
The exiled are always waiting for the separation to begin,
suddenly, the trees are stylized, Italian.

The animals know this presence, are changed
into an impatient fear, subtle knocking around.
And this angel doesn't have bird wings exactly
but something waxy, the ability to move
through time as if it were a place.

Think of the future as the middle ages and all its stone
and smoke and darkness, the droughts, the impossible
        weather,
the nights banged down like a helmet over the head,
so much to be done! She is so ordinary,
she is beautiful.
Memory is an omen when
the world opens its green mouth like a child,
hungry beyond any description we will ever have.
The ordinary flutterings from within she feels
God taking stubborn root in the natural world.

Adam & Eve

I.
If she said nothing stirred in her it would have been a lie.
She was a firm believer in the real. Imagine—the two of
        them,
loitering in those awkward adolescent bodies. This passion
between them, a revelation—of course—like a passage
        written
and forgotten for centuries and found in some lost scroll, a
        song
to take to prison. The hush of thousands upon thousands
of acres of dry grass blowing, the sunlight provoking,
something no one can take from you.
It didn't start casually.
Instead it was her timid Greek smile. It was reaction
to the protraction of darkness.

There could be no rescue
just as we may not talk to the dead one last time.
The deer moved through the amplification of light,
        unraveling
beyond the lush maze of swamp, past the fussing birds—
what we would later call *that fiddling of nature.*

The voice of instruction was after all something she thought
she thought, conscience made real. Fireflies lifting from the
        dense
grass and flowers of the meadow, the natural slope of the
        hill up.
There was a shadow-figure far away—a darkness
they imagined barely survivable. This all happened

before we could bring faraway things up close.
Isn't it our nature to explore—to mistrust darkness?

There was a particular hillside, wood ducks in a ruckus,
the moon just a dream, for once something to point at,
something sometimes complete. And even thousands of
        years
later there would be a rough approximation of these two
        figures,
looking out into the distance for clarification, movement—
significance. How can there be choice without memory?
How can there be sin without childhood?

II.

It is now much later and my lover says to me,
Imagine nothing and touches my hair, *not light,*
not the void because that is something
he whispers *undo, undo, undo.*
The sun seems like a mirror, training a heat on us,
burning our clothes of paper.

Driving through the inner city, through the dusk of late
      November
past schoolchildren in uniforms pressing forward
toward home, I occasionally remember what time is
to the child—how an hour in the kitchen alone is
      as long as
a day's drive through the midwest—
and I occasionally see an old lot that has been neglected
long enough, a car dealership, or unused playground that
has been reclaimed by nature. There are huge weeds,
      tall as trees,
wild unlacing the blacktop, cement. Then,
I imagine our cities taken back, vined over, undone.

III.

That original landscape was establishing a tenderness, but
      that was
myth, metaphor, and if in fact perfect—quickly taken away.
There in the suddenly ruined world was the bird
eating the bug, *a punctuation*.
The lion pausing at blood-smeared rib cage
of a gazelle, *acceptable hunger*.

There were the trees, the edge of the rock hill and lashed
      to it,
cypress, eucalyptus, olive and palm.
This was the apprenticeship to loneliness.
And after he withdrew from her, the world's first tears.

Isn't there a point in all our lives when we stand
at the top of the basement stairs and watch our fathers burn
everything of value in the furnace?

He imagines the children have suddenly substituted their
      love
for him with a passion for each other. It isn't that way—but
      appears so.
Then, the sky rolled blank, huge herds materialized,
      roaming
the boundaries in the rocky hills as the sun came up
      overhead.

The joke: eternity is a long time.
I am Eve in that moment when I find myself alone,
at the door, the sun so bright it is blinding even though it
        is raining.
I raise my hand to shield my eyes. Always behind the
        landscape—
the obedience of hope. The woman standing
at the screen door is sobbing,
the magnolia losing its opulent blossoms in the walls of rain,
the creamy petals browning under the faint touch of winds.
I remember the church as my childhood—that is what she
        thinks.
It is the most obscure of gifts, our second nature really,
and the thing we learn over and over to suppress—
a gentle kindness, a hope.

Swans

Long after the first drinks of the afternoon
the sun slumps into the willows behind the house.
The cook must be arranging a duck on a platter, fussing
with blooming garnishes.
Someone played the flute in the yard yesterday
and that melody hangs, a heat in the wild iris.
There is the daughter marching back and forth,
wearing bare the grass at the edge of the cliff
overlooking the Hudson. She is trying to imagine
the land unmanicured—before settlement, before
the first Europeans came drifting down the river,
paddles paused—a concert of sunlight, loud and violent
going down, drowning right ahead.

This is the world of any good landscape painter.
Her father is slouching in the cane chair, trying to talk
with her while he plays chess with an imaginary friend.
He throws questions and she rolls her eyes, kicks pebbles
down the bank to an end he cannot hear.
This man wants his daughter.
He wants her so much that he is unable to stop the
            others—
the hand at the breast which is stippled with goose bumps,
her face always focused on a point beyond the heavy
            weight
anchoring above her—the older men, her father's cronies.

She turns and tells him, *I have learned to expect nothing*.
He starts to weep. He loves her.
His face is scarlet from coughing. A dark ivory pawn

is tossed, then a bishop toward the water. She keeps pacing,
browsing the edge of what is his, looking at the
          landscape—
Those trees are so thick, dense
and lush—and she is in a pale dress envisioning the large
          quiet ponds
of Connecticut.

When the father finally rises to wash for dinner, greet
          guests,
she realizes perhaps for the first time it is his death she is
          after.
She opens the door to the shed, and is slapped with the
          coolness
and there are blocks of ice on the floor, sawdust, the odor
of cedar and dozens of white swans hanging there
like huge abstract question marks.
Their necks glow, the feathers of the 1800s seem to
          phosphor
below those huge but delicate webbed feet in the slush
of darkness that overtakes the day. The floor is a wash of
          blood
and it is her father's death soon in coming
when his heart will simply unlace itself
like a dark ribbon that will buoy her, buoyed.

The Tub

I sit on the green silk bank of the stream
watching a group of Canada geese fret over three small
      goslings.
Behind me, the road takes its turn,
empty, just a place for a fox to run along in the open.

The mountains in the distance are pewter—
like the pitcher, cool and sweating on my grandmother's
      lace
tablecloth. The barn next to the house,
I know what it contains:
rows and rows of pigeons, shifting on the thick beams
near the roof. When the light has only one thing left to do,
to fall into itself,
the birds will move out
over the fields, churning the sky.

In the white house behind me, in a deserted kitchen,
there is a woman, nude, crouched in a tin tub—
knee-deep in water
in a shaft of early evening sunlight which falls
across her back like ash.

Egypt in Flaubert's Time

for Molly Bendall

The moon dilates over the water
and the few imaginary ducks turn their heads
back on themselves, over the thick feathers, folding up
for the night. The double doors to the balcony are open,
a bottle of something imported on the desk
and a smile of satisfaction on her face.
The type of expression that one has
when everything depends on being believed—the
      expression
flushing a face after several drinks.

She is writing a letter to a cousin
who will slice open the envelope with a knife
months from now. *There is something sad about the women*
walking in the moonlight along the river basin,
their darkly wrapped figures, the shuffle of sandals, the dust,
the late night exhale of breeze off the river.
And it seems odd, on some nights the shoreline *seems*
as if it could have been photographed by the light of the
      moon . . .

The boats on the Nile are long and slender,
the sails bound down and wrapped. The palm trees shoot
up from the shore—like exclamation marks—they are what
she sees first, what comes up
in the photographic pain in the darkness, like at night,
the dark folds between the leaves, the spaces where the
      sharp

foliage overlaps. She hears a bird cry
sharp as a paper cut.

Perspective darkens, she tells this cousin, whispers
as if she were next to her not weeks away, away
like winter is to summer in the clogged French garden.
During the day, she goes into the desert, this strange
premonition of a woman, so out of place in the white
Victorian costume, and mixes the sticky substance which
she spreads perfectly in one stroke on the surface
of the glass plate in a tent laboratory where the temperature
reaches one hundred and twenty.
At night she forgets she has been sent away,
forgets the fever of her fingers over a piano.
She walks along the stone alleys, past walls, fingering
the impressions, like a blind woman, like a romantic—

running her fingers along the thin forms, the squatting
symbols, the figures of kings.
There are things she realizes are unimaginable,
that is what she says, she has learned here
the way the ancient Egyptians could not have imagined
the gothic head

to come thousands of years later,
the expressive line between the lips,
the head that began with tears.

The Middle Ages

As she left the market by the sea
the farmers released a herd of hogs
into a stand of oak to feed on dropped acorns under a pile
of hurried clouds. To come back here is to forget:
the pigs move through a shower of sunlight,
making a thrush over downed leaves.
A conversation passes, like wine between men,
a cackle of laughter falling—
sticks breaking and a joke that wouldn't apply, translate,
      now.
Two dogs chase between the nearby birches,
crows start angry possessive taunt, cries dropping
in flight, limb to branch over the dumb dogs.

A young woman walks the road.
She has a pouch of salt and several stiff fish.
She thinks of a barn as volatile,
how summer afternoons can lead heat high,
then imagines heat crowding like a procession of storm
      clouds
near the rafters above the stacks of bound bronze grass.

Almost home she sees the moon, an ancient, classical moon,
rise big as a body of water, a body—
behind the tips of trees.
The branches wag in the wind, the pale sky.
A chill comes to the woman's back like music,
moves like a finger tracing her spine, the start of something.
Night hammers into place overhead.
In bed, while she is being touched, a ridge of sandy hills

surfaces, she remembers the shore.
Cows passed slowly. How the waves looked tin-colored,
jubilant, and the small boats tossed about under
the brooding sunlight!

The Fire's Hypnotic Flickering

Camille Claudel became a pupil of Rodin's at nineteen and
would later become his model, muse and collaborator. For
almost a decade she left her mark on many of Rodin's
masterpieces while at the same time producing sculptures of
her own. When Rodin refused to marry her, Camille ended
their relationship and struggled in poverty to continue her
own work until finally her family committed her to an
asylum for the insane, where she remained for thirty years
until her death.

CAMILLE CLAUDEL 1864–1943

I.
The lovers have closed their eyes
The woman is leaning off the stool toward the man
kneeling in front of her   *If there were movement*
he would be   crawling up her kissing her cheek
crawling on top of her like summer crawls on top of spring
But there isn't movement   his back
is a lovely arch   *ache*
it is a swoon of marble
Everything is music in the end   isn't it
Just as when one is confused by whose hand is whose
and two bodies
piece together perfectly so that
there isn't really an edge of light between them
making stone fluid making stone defy its own definition
that is what I was interested in   *always*
the waltz you know
the way two bodies lean into each other and gain
a momentum that one alone couldn't attain or sustain
manufacture

II.

I posed and composed   *lending my body*
to more than one damned soul—*lending my body*
Just as when one is confused by whose hand is whose
during the festival of passion   There will be people
who will later recognize my hands, my feet, the gestures
as a fragment of my world   *Often it was my face*
undone and redone   that pout of recognition
which quickly turns itself into that moan
that cry   at the edge of that cliff   the only cliff
at the end of the world
everyone will utter the same thing   *no   no   no*
No repeated so many times that it becomes just a rhythm
the sound coming from machinery or an ocean
that seems to repeat and repeat finally just becoming
        background

III.

I'll tell you what women know
We know how to distract
And we know how often the astonished man
forgets his own source   that his idea
was something he should have remembered hearing
not thinking
But he remembers thinking it
I didn't just lose my mind
Maybe there were babies I had to give away
Maybe there really were spies sneaking into my studio
at night doing sketches for someone else
Maybe there were too many cats
and not enough food
And maybe my family didn't know what to do
with me, a woman, a daughter and sister who buys stone
instead of bread or pears
Maybe there were some men who really wanted me
sent away silent

IV.

Suddenly   I see the trick of the universe
the trick is to keep the big questions out of context
hidden or reduced
turning away is as bad as committing a crime
Watching someone else sign their name to something
your own hands have fashioned into a flame
You know the tree stump which has been worried
by the weather into a bulb of flame
There are dead cedars in the distance
hills holding up the sky—
and I thought early
that love
was a kind of clarity!

There is nothing called the art of argument
because that implies an attitude of persuasion
as if truth had anything to do
with persuasion   with
a young woman at her dressing table   a young Roman
a group of good-natured gossipers
a young woman with a sheaf

When we reach the gates of hell
it is always early in the medieval morning
then will we realize perspective is not just the term
for space in an architect's drawing
then will you too be asking for another chance
with my mouth
and the hands you will raise   will be mine

Three

Balance is only rhythm, the swing
in the swing
of the pendulum,
neither loss nor possession—
—JoEllen Kwiatek

What Is Beyond Us

FOR TIM

Above the meadow of pain, and pins of Queen Anne's lace,
black-eyed Susans and tall silver grass, the moon lifts large,
      white,
a lake.
The midwife instructs me to remember something pleasant.
She is raising her voice, calling my name.
I don't remember anything.
My grandfather and I played a game called, *hand over hand*.
First, he placed his large hand palm down on the tablecloth,
my hand went on top, our hands alternating till we had a
      little hill
of hands. The hand on the bottom was pulled out and
      slapped
on the top of the stack—and so it went.
We played till our hands were a blur, till dinner.
Tickle, tickle on your knee, if you laugh you don't love me.

I don't believe this. I don't believe this.
That's what I tell you, my voice a dark wing moving
      over us.
I am on a sailboat, standing on the bow, looking ahead,
spotting for rocks, shallow water, a ridge of sand. We drift
past the jetty of rocks, past the marina, the stranded skipjack
of boyscouts who wave and laugh with embarrassment.
I'm in a dinghy alone, on my knees, paddling to shore,
past birches and scrub pine.
Near the beach the lilies' closed white fists float on the
      surface

of the water. Two herons pedal and rise into the sky.
The air is pink, the water violet-green.
The midwife tells me, think of pain as constructive.

This pain is the best kept secret in the world.
My father died late at night, young and alone in some
        hospital
after drinking and drinking. Your father came from Ireland
in the late twenties and even when he had the chance,
didn't return. We suppose he wanted to return too badly
and like a man who loves a woman too much, he pushes
        her away.
I'm not remembering any of this because I'm on an
        opposite shore,
under hectic moon, the birches just doors of moonlight.

I am in a darkness I won't remember.

This is the best kept secret in the world;
we've dropped anchor, the low clouds are, in the almost
        darkness
the color of pearls. There are acres of reeds, a few startled
        birds,
trees. And when they hand you the child,
our daughter, you look at me with a face I've never seen
        before;
I've heard, sometimes, it's what we've never seen before
that we recognize.

The Back Room

for Emmy Nesbitt

The first time you saw a man and woman making love
you were eight. It was morning, the sunlight battering the
    snow.
You stood there caught in the doorway, holding the
    doorknob
as my lover shrank from me.
Your mother sent you upstairs for my lack of a clock
and the instruction was not to open the door
to the back room but to knock and say the time.

Months later you sauntered up to me outside,
the fields were thawing under a pale gush of light
and below the confusion of weeping willow
the stream was full of noise.
You whispered, *I never want to wear a white dress.*

You said this through cupped hands at my ear,
forsythia blurred to a flame in the ditch near the road.
At first I didn't know what you meant, but then
memory welled up in me strong as the need to weep.
His hand on my shoulder, his breath past my ear,
the window-seat bed.

I told you you would like it.
I tried to explain the pleasure of love's exhaustion,
losing one's self in the body, the want of the little death,
the split second with the forgotten self.

Now, you are older and I am married to someone else.
All afternoon your mother and I watched you stand
with a boy down by the creek,
the cows moved by behind you, purposeless as dark clouds;
the sun sputtered on the horizon, a horn.

And later as I walk with you home from the dump
on the dirt road, following the unused red railroad tracks
we come upon them—two moths facing each other
like lovers, like petals, against huge brown
iridescent fans of fungus overtaking a mushy stump.

Their wings petals, each decorated
with an unearthly eye.
And this reminds you of when I was first pregnant.
In those first few months when you went with me to the
        midwife.
We watched the child inside me twist and tumble,
backbone just a comb projected on that screen
in that dark room.

That month the textbook described the baby the size
and weight of a moth . . .
the next month, a letter
heavy as a envelope, later still
a Spanish onion, a telephone receiver and on and on.

And as we squat here, prodding
these insects, these two abstractions of what is vital,
waiting for them to light, as if blown
like opulent blossoms—off following nocturnal habits

through the lattice of leaves—
I remember how shortly after my daughter was born
I thought of you. Your old fear . . .
the white dress of sex, the window-seat bed.

You had already entered that land without fear,
the province of the body.
My husband was tired, sitting by the bed,
the baby in his arms.
She was staring at the lights, the clock, the world
        exhausted.
And that is when I realized,
I lied to you years before out of ignorance.
How that becomes this!

One Version

Your brother delivers meat on a big, ancient English bicycle
through the snowy streets past the bakeries of old Chicago.
It is late afternoon and the music from the radio is a gesture
thrown at evening. There is the smell of dinner, potatoes—
even brisket and your desire just recently to be of use.
Your father is sick, has been. But today it seems sudden
and you are taken with the seriousness of it.
You are thinking that this is different than you thought
it would be. This is like a child thinking if you poured
water into a glass and poured past the rim
that the water would retain, would keep
the shape of that juice glass.
It is that kind of stupid disappointment—
the mind's resistance to believe is real.
It is expecting something ridiculous—something miraculous
from the real world . . . the way youth always expects
its literal house will be spared, will be the exception.
The shadows between the houses are more solid
than the apartment buildings themselves.
Your father has to go to the hospital
and this is the day you realize you look like him,
you have his body.

Your mother tells you—*you are strong enough*
even though he is incredibly tall, with the bones
of a man who could work. You look at your hands,
he's called them *dressmaker's*.
You walk to the top of the stairs carrying him,
a quaking thing. You stand there balancing your father
realizing you cannot get him down those stairs.

46

He is crying, pleading. He doesn't want to go.
He has grabbed the banister. You can't believe this—
trying to undo his fingers from the polished wood . . .
this memory later will be stubborn as gravity, reliable
this falling back to clarify, and hard to believe as seeing a
       ghost.
This is the beginning, it all happens in increments.
It is the beginning, but it is yourself, not your father, you
       fear for.
Because you know as you hold him,
one arm behind your father's warm neck, the other
under his huge knees, that when your father finally dies—
his death will take you from yourself
like a big, fast Russian sleigh
with a loud confusion of bells
through an anthology of nights.

Nocturne: Little Cottage After Midnight

Because we drank too much and were out of practice
because of the baby I woke up well after midnight for
          water
in that banished silence, the well of deep night, no distant
cars slurring a distant corner or even dogs barking . . .
then fell back to sleep instantly. I had a dream, that
          something
was at the window, like a lantern, or a limb—maybe a bird,
maybe a hummingbird. But this is what made it a dream—
it was like an apparition of something coming. I dreamt
then of the idea, the thing becoming a verb—fluttering
at the end of the room. Just moonlight interrupted by
          frantic
beating—pulse of wings. I was sleeping the sleep of those
          drowned,
those loved, of those exhausted, nude. But it was real
          movement
over my face, like a hand dragging,
a piece of goldenrod snapping back with no scent.

Sleeping still, I was like those sleeping outdoors centuries
          ago.
And I knew, suddenly, that it was not your hand dragging
          over my cheek—
it was something I didn't recognize, strange. I scuttled out
          of bed,
half moaning, yelling, *something is in here.* And that is when
you screamed the guttural scream of a man who thinks
          there is
a robber climbing through the window: yelling, *stop* or *no.*

It was the unfamiliar voice, your voice, that woke you.
We see that it's a bat. You thought it was a person, thought
I said, *someone*. The closet door is open and the bat circles
the room under the light. You put on a shirt. You find a
      broom.
It takes an hour to kill.

When we return to bed, you will dream you are
your father. And you won't believe how accomplished you
      feel—
think of the pines as *sheltering*
the daffodils as *wet*
stars declarations of something large like math
we are exiles on a train being brought out of a dangerous
      country
this wind a kind of seasonal surrender
the field the bat has brought us to
a psalm
the natural world

Consider the man who never marries—who takes
a cane chair out into the finished field but never lives
in the natural world.
Think of the man who never protects his wife—never
catches a salmon, starts a fire from scraps, never builds
anything from wood.

You are your father and I am your father's lover.
This is your dream. This is what you watch.
Our daughter sleeping in the next room *is you* sometimes.
You care about her as you care about yourself.

It is the kind of sleep where the love trade heads—
trick photography—the confusion of the mirror.
And you watch your father (you watch yourself)
save his lover from the hand, what she thinks is the hand,
quick and frightening as wings.

December

. . . we're to be given no heaven,
No heaven   but this

              —DAVID ST. JOHN

This is the unimaginable present,
here between Thanksgiving and Christmas.
The day stretches and a waterman upriver unravels
a whole flock of dark decoys onto the surface of the cold
      water,
trailing them out behind a workboat.
Two figures walk out onto a neighboring pier
because the day is unseasonable, warm.
The old waterman and his son gun the engine
of the low white workboat, cutting a wake to open water.
On the neighboring pier our figures turn into a couple—
and the couple begins to fight,
gesturing, each so obviously exhausted by the other's tale.
They are outside themselves watching, but being objective
doesn't help them. They still cast the wrong accusations
at great expense, harm.
Now the lovers have bowed their heads &
are beyond words, empty.
Fortunately, the light is a logic establishing
an order, everything shining in a yolk of blasted light,
evergreen, poinsettia in the window, eagle, shrew.

Across the river the stripped trees release the faraway echo
of that workboat, slipping through the channel to open
      water
toward the wild inlets on the other side.

Reconciliation is always what we hope for, a natural act—
the light, the land and the tide's years of collaboration—
that is what our lovers hope for.
And then, during their hoping, they see them:
the two mallards, each duck bobbing its head
and paddling in circles around the other.

Suddenly, the male mounts the female
and bites her neck; she looks like she is drowning &
this is funny, the notion of the duck dying, drowning in
   water—
So that the lovers are reminded of each other.
They are reminded that happiness
is a tentative thing.
Take them back. Take them back
to when love was just the body's thoughtless response.

The Dreams

Night arrives solid and heavy,
more than several blocks long, to displace
its weight and float like a tanker over us.

It is because my husband is from the Midwest
that he dreams of twisters. Every spring in his head
he is running to beat the wind.
Sometimes a child again
he is at the dining room table overseeing
an arrangement of baseball cards.
Interrupting that satisfied moment, a sudden darkness,
false night. It is as if the moon slid its face
in front of the sun and beyond the window—leaves,
limbs, garbage can lids fly by, horizontal.
He hears his dead father's cough from the next room,
his father's slippers hit the floor and rush for the screen
         door.
A garage three doors down is lifted, picked up and turned
ninety degrees, placed back down on its foundation.
This is power—indiscriminate, unexpected—
slicing the afternoon in half.

He is always racing against the odds—trying to
run fast through knee-deep water, hide in the cellar
close a blown window,
latch a gate,

the funnel cloud eating a path toward him.
The other night, I had a dream
and being from the East I have never thought

about what a tornado could undo—
the sky turned green along a cliff of clouds.
Green the queer pea-soup haze painted
behind Moses in the childhood Bible.
My husband and I were in the country, under this high sky.
And in this dream we were living in the farmhouse,
he was with me in my former life.
The winter wheat shimmered, grasped the draining light
and turned to water.

In the distance the funnel unhitches from its backdrop of
          hills
and we watch the tornado skate across the fields of the
          Amish.
We are stopped on the dirt road, frozen as everything
around us unlatches and shakes, convulses in the wind.
Suddenly the color fades from the scene;
this is black-and-white as any good science-fiction show.
Trees fall to their knees, huge broccoli tops.
There is the strange lane of destruction, the flattened
          chicken coop,
the neighbor's mobile home shredded lettuce on the lawn.
We are untouched, the barn proud.
And here, I see the world for what it is—
see the scene my lover sees and fears—the world undressed
of illusion, frail, the line of destruction crazy, a zigzag path.
One side havoc and the other side, nothing
but the normal unbraided cornfield.

The numerals of darkness fade between the houses.
And just as the lover is supposed to mirror the loved

and vice versa—just as my past is *his*—
beyond the exchanging of rings—taking on the other's
      fears,
living them as your own nightmares
under the vaulted sky,
the sun advancing to declare the day.

White Place in Shadow

FOR MY DAUGHTER, KATHERINE

Realism is sometimes not what we recognize.
I mean, those violets on the windowsill, copper pots
hanging over the stove, the blue bloom of gas shuddering
under the teapot, wood stacked for a fire, sticks to get it
      going—
all give the impression life is solid, survivable.
But I must admit sometimes—like those lovers of literature
who are always looking for symbolism, the meaning,
more meaning than there really is—I forget the story
in favor of the idea.
The story is the story.
My hope is that it is as it seems—the world
like the test, you know, for color blindness—surely
there is a recognizable numeral or letter, symbol
placed within the haphazard splatter?
It is midmorning and there is that relay of light,
autumnal, trees staggering at the edge of the dirt path,
sunlight at its odd, low angle making the woods appear
less dense. It is the beginning of fall and the clouds
are frilly—huge—baroque.
Later, although I don't know it now,
my daughter and I will put sunglasses and a hat
on the dog and laugh and the sun will trot over the horizon
fast as a horse.

This is the day I realize, there is no going back.
Walking from my daughter's bedroom I hear the
      high-pitched

narration while she plays before sleep.
She instructs Mickey to kiss the elephant,
and reaching the kitchen I listen to the loud, exaggerated
imaginary kiss between the two plastic figures pushed
         together.
This child has a high fever and is supposed to be kept
quiet—
But it was just moments ago in the bedroom
as she coughed and tossed, her face mottled,
flushed and splotchy that she pulled me by the collar
with a strength one wouldn't expect
till my face was just inches from hers, mirroring,
and said, *I don't want to die.*

I asked her, *How did you find out about death?*
I actually asked her, *Who told you?*

Letter from the Modern World

FOR JOELLEN KWIATEK

He hated his life & now it is over
and you drive to tell your sister & while you travel
past perishing green fields, past light so stunning
you could weep at its reprieve—
you think of your father's girlfriend with the red hair,
the one he took off with to Florida, to live with near
the dog tracks, after he left the family for something
       different.
His death comes to you like a rumor, light replaced
by something moving over the fields, like some huge beast
dragging its shadow & grazing. You know the sky has fallen
a notch, that you are Chicken-Little. You know he is dead
before the phone actually rings.

When your father spoke to you,
it was always with the authority of the *posthumous whisper*—
the aloofness of one in exile—and then the fierce gaze.
And now, you are struck like flint by stone.
He is light, fluid as poured water.

It could be argued that the love of the world,
that engagement, begins with the memorizing
of a parent's body. The first fierce attachment has to do
with notice, knowing another's body. Remember your
       mother's body—
her slip, stockinged feet, her face just after sleep softened it,
the bedclothes, her rings & then the hands
whose veins your fingers traced—first palm side down,

then in love and boredom, over to the pulse and up
past the wrist till the blood's route disappeared in the flesh
of her upper arm. She will always be the woman who
        loved him,
the woman he loved.

Remember, then, your father's body—the weight of him—
the body you want now returned, shipped north.
Remember his hankie which he pulled out maybe more
        than once
to weep into, then folded & placed back in his pocket.
Remember his body, the scars on his body, and how
they were not modern. How he held a cigarette in the dark
        living room
night after night
while the rest of the house slept.
He drank through the bleak hours like a traveler
who is just thirsty waiting it out
between dark countries.

Now think of your parents' bed. Consider the white sheets,
the open door to the room, the window & behind it the
        sky
which was a ravine to fall into during the long sluggish days
        of childhood,
waiting for snow, waiting for the snow to end.
The sun a condolence, haloed in the milky sky.
And on the bed, the sheets enthralled with each other,
        drapery
at its bottom—so beautiful it reminds us of stone, a frieze,
        art.

This is the glance backward. Oh, the stodginess of real life!
Gravity made visible, for even as children we knew
people were planted in their lives.
The snow shovel, the shed, the gestured trees, the ocean so
bright and busy it is blinding, and the mother forever
        waiting,
watching out the kitchen window for the father.
There was always a window, a map
a detail of possibilities elsewhere—this was childhood,
& the fantasies of the future, detailed as embroidery.
The solution was to keep walking, keep walking home
        from church,
from school, from houses other than your own.

Now, suddenly, for the first time the distant hills are not a
        place
to walk into. The time it takes to draw a
        bath—insufferable;
This grief is malignant.
You want a definition for your dead father: before
the new world, when one could have a soul,
when people weren't only what they did.
You think of the past & remember wanting to go for a ride
in the country. You wanted to get lost.

You want to say:
Give me the old European city, a body which is dead and
        dressed,
coins for my father's tired eyes—snow piled at the edge of a
        narrow
road, an alley of stone or brick,

a winter sky suspended with smoke, the promise of snow,
a white oblivion, an early darkness, a cemetery crammed
       into the center
of a small, noisy town, a black iron fence, antique trees,
grave diggers using axes because the ground refuses,
       drunken men,
diggers resigned to eternity.

Give me workers to pass on the way to bury the body,
men in smocks repairing a gutter, someone carrying a
       broken clock,
a boy delivering a cake, a girl with a beautiful face
watching for the cake from a second-story window, her
       face
just a shadow above us. Give me painters painting
& carrying ladders, a scene before the modern world as we
       know it—
when two domestics met for love in the back pantry
every other afternoon in the house beside the church.

Give me clergy in robes who dream in Latin, give me a
       town
that comes out & weeps at the edge of the road, a butcher
with a gesture of blood flung across his fat front,
a tailor who is nearsighted with pins in his mouth &
silence in his heart, a blacksmith.

Give me animals with those huffy breaths
& heavy footfalls, a dark carriage to walk behind, all my
       sisters
and mother in black, our faces veiled, our vision erased

by grief. The only noise would be a coach leaving, a
         conductor's voice
announcing the villages along the proposed route as if the
         towns
themselves were for sale and he were the auctioneer.
Give me a pageant that interrupts

the commerce of one single day for my father's passage
out over the dark water into the frigid air
toward the incalculable stars.
Give me an enemy more recognizable than time,
than our failure to make use of history,
his story—
than the failure of character,
the impossibility of one man's survival in the modern
         world.